Jun 2016

D1126484

PIRATES AROUND THE WORLD

Terror on the High Seas

Sir Francis Drake

Don Nardo

Mitchell Lane
PUBLISHERS
P.O. Box 196
Hockessin, DE 19707
www.mitchelllane.com

PUBLISHERS

Printing   1   2   3   4   5   6   7   8

Anne Bonny
Black Bart (Bartholomew Roberts)
Blackbeard (Edward Teach)
François L'Olonnais

Long Ben (Henry Every)
Sir Francis Drake
Sir Henry Morgan
William Kidd

Library of Congress Cataloging-in-Publication Data
Nardo, Don, 1947–
 Sir Francis Drake / by Don Nardo.
     pages cm. — (Pirates around the world: terror on the high seas)
 Includes bibliographical references and index.
 Audience: Grades 3-6.
 ISBN 978-1-68020-044-7 (library bound)
 1. Drake, Francis, 1540?–1596—Juvenile literature. 2. Great Britain—History, Naval—Tudors, 1485–1603—Biography—Juvenile literature
 3. Great Britain—History—Elizabeth, 1558–1603—Biography—Juvenile literature. 4. Explorers—Great Britain—Biography—Juvenile literature.
 5. Admirals—Great Britain—Biography—Juvenile literature. I. Title.
 DA86.22.D7N37 2015
 942.05'5092—dc23
 [B]
                                                                    2015003195

eBook ISBN: 978-1-68020-045-4

Contents

Words in **bold** throughout can be found in the Glossary.

Introduction
Betrayal and a Longing for Revenge

Thousands of miles from home, Francis Drake found himself facing total disaster and a painful death. He and his cousin, John Hawkins, had set sail from Plymouth, England, in early October 1567 with a small fleet of six ships. Hawkins was captain of the *Minion* and Drake commanded the *Judith*.

Some people felt that Drake, now just in his mid-twenties, was a bit young to be a captain. To attain that important job usually required a lot of time and experience at sea. But Drake was no ordinary sailor. A Portuguese seaman wrote, "He is one of the greatest sailors in the world, both in his skill and his command of men . . . he treats all of his men with affection, and they treat him with respect."[1] Part of that respect came from Drake's obvious mastery of the art of sailing. That was why the older, more established captain, Hawkins, had felt safe in entrusting him with a ship.

A Privateer, Not a Pirate!

In the months following its departure, the fleet skirted Africa's western coast. In stop after stop, Hawkins and Drake obtained black Africans and chained them in the holds of their ships. This practice was part of the awful slave trade that was beginning to take shape. The vessels brought valuable goods from Europe—including fine fabrics, iron tools, and gunpowder—to villages on the African coast. In exchange, local tribal chiefs swapped their own slaves, who had often been captured from neighboring tribes. Sometimes the Europeans kidnapped unprotected black villagers. Then the ships carried the captives across the Atlantic to European colonies in the Americas.

The unfortunate Africans who had been ripped from their homes and way of life became slaves in those colonies. At that time, most European settlements in the region belonged to Spain. In fact, Spain had so many colonies in South America, Mexico, and the Caribbean islands that they formed an overseas empire, nicknamed the "Spanish Main."

England was often at war with Spain. It was not unusual for English ships to raid the Spanish Main. Officials in Spain frequently called those raiders "pirates," a term Drake resented and rejected. He pointed out that a pirate was a dishonorable criminal. Pirates, he said, assaulted vessels and towns and stole money and other valuables.

Drake instead called himself a **privateer**. In a sense privateers were a legal and morally acceptable kind of pirate. They had the consent of their king or queen to raid an enemy's ships and towns. Drake and Hawkins argued they were privateers because their queen, Elizabeth I, backed their ventures.

An Unexpected Trap

When they left Plymouth in 1567, however, Drake and Hawkins did not intend to attack the Spanish colonies. They wanted to trade with them instead. The cousins' main goal was to get rich by selling the black captives they acquired in Africa.

To that end, the six English ships entered the harbor of San Juan de Ulúa, a Spanish colony on Mexico's eastern coast. Drake and Hawkins told the local authorities that they wanted supplies. They also needed to make minor repairs to their vessels. While this was happening, Hawkins said, the Englishmen desired to trade. In exchange for gold or other valuables, they would be glad to supply local landowners with black slaves.

At first, the Spaniards were reluctant to trade. Drake and Hawkins had no permits from the Spanish government to conduct commerce with Spain's colonies, they said. Clearly, Hawkins told Drake, these individuals needed some "convincing." It took the form of the English ships aiming their cannons at the nearby town. Not surprisingly, the Spanish officials got the message and announced they were ready to begin trading.

Before the parties started **negotiating**, however, the situation suddenly changed. According to a noted modern expert on Drake, Hans P. Kraus, a fleet "of thirteen great ships sailed into the harbor, with the new governor of Mexico, Don Martin Enriquez, on board."[2] These vessels were heavily armed with their own cannons. Drake and Hawkins were badly outnumbered. Moreover, they were trapped in the harbor.

"After a few days of negotiations," Kraus continues, "a pact was concluded." This agreement allowed the English "to

A 1620 drawing of John Hawkins.

repair their ships and purchase ashore the supplies they needed." Meanwhile, "the Spanish ships would anchor near them."[3]

Harboring a Hatred

Drake and Hawkins initially thought they had caught a lucky break. But they soon realized they were dead wrong. According to a surviving Spanish document, the governor did not feel bound to honor "an agreement made with raiders . . . he decided to fight them, and ordered a considerable number of soldiers" to prepare to fire upon the English. "This was done, and the guns of the fleet bombarded the English ships."[4]

Soon, the harbor was transformed into a mass of firing cannons, explosions, blinding smoke, and screaming and dying men. Four English ships were destroyed.

The *Judith* wasn't one of them. It appears that Drake thought his cousin's ship, the *Minion*, had been overwhelmed and wrecked. So he wasted no time in fleeing. Thanks to his skill and courage, the *Judith* made it out of the harbor. What Drake did not realize was that Hawkins was very much alive and his ship was still intact. Hawkins also managed to escape. Assuming that Drake had abandoned him, Hawkins was hurt and angry. "The *Judith* deserted us in our great misery,"[5] he later said. He thereafter held a grudge against Drake.

The incident resulted in a second, much more deep-rooted, grudge. Drake harbored a hatred for the Spanish governor, Don Martin Enriquez. His **treachery** had resulted in the deaths of hundreds of English sailors. From then on, he had a longing to get revenge on the man—and the nation—who had betrayed him.

1591

SIC PARVIS MAGNA

This sixteenth-century painting of Sir Francis Drake captures his confident air.

Learning to Be a Ship's Captain

Like many aspects of Francis Drake's life, the date of his birth is not known for certain. Modern scholars think it was sometime between 1540 and 1544. More certain is his birthplace—Tavistock, a town in the county of Devon, in southwestern England.

At the time of his birth, English Catholics and Protestants were strongly at odds. Devon and the surrounding region composed a mainly Catholic stronghold. Francis's father, Edmund Drake, was a Protestant preacher who hated not only Catholics but also Spaniards simply because they were Catholics. As a result, the boy came to despise nearly all things Catholic and Spanish.

Little is known about the family outside of the father and his famous son. It appears that Edmund's wife's name was Margerie. Also, their children may have numbered as few as three or as many as twelve.

Home in Floating Hulk

Whatever the family's size, it resided in the rotting hull of an old sailing ship in Plymouth harbor. This floating hulk still had its masts. Little Francis spent much of his time climbing them. He "raced across the old weather-beaten decks," Drake's biographer Chelsea Curtis wrote. "And when night would come he often fell asleep" amid

the gentle movements of "the tide and the lullaby of the sailors' songs."[1]

The elder Drake was not shy about expressing his anti-Catholic views. This incited loud and fierce reactions from Devon's many Catholics. Fearing for his family's safety, Edmund moved them to the largely Protestant county of Kent.

Edmund Drake quickly made a name for himself as a preacher. Soon the government took notice and asked him to lead local sailors of the Royal Navy in prayer. But the job did not pay very well. Therefore, Edmund sent Francis to sea when he was thirteen so there would be fewer mouths to feed.

The boy became an assistant to the captain of a cargo ship. That seasoned seaman taught young Francis a great deal. The two became fast friends. When the captain died, he left the vessel to the young man, who was then about eighteen. Drake soon sold the ship. Exactly what he did with the money is unknown.

An Urge to Go to Sea

What *is* known is that Drake wanted to become a rich sea captain. During his teens he witnessed hundreds of captains itching for adventure and wealth. Spain had been steadily expanding its far-flung and wealthy overseas empire in the Americas. So one way for a captain to achieve success was to raid Spanish ships and colonies. Ripe for the taking were large stores of gold, silver, silk, linen, pearls, precious gems, and fine wines.

Most of these ship captains were out-and-out pirates. But a few had the blessing of Queen Elizabeth. Drake hoped to meet her and acquire her backing.

At some point in the early 1560s, Drake got that chance when he began working for Hawkins. The Hawkins family also lived in Plymouth. John led a group of well-to-do merchants who made their fortunes by pirating from the Spanish, French, and others. Strictly speaking, much of what they did was against the law. But the English government usually turned a blind eye to it.

In 1564, Queen Elizabeth awarded Hawkins an official permit to launch a trading expedition. The main cargo his ships would carry was slaves. Buying and/or capturing black slaves from western Africa was becoming a **lucrative** business. And both the queen and Hawkins wanted to benefit from it. While today making someone a slave is often regarded as a terrible and cruel crime, slavery was accepted as a necessary fact of life in that era.

Drake accompanied Hawkins on the trip as his second-in-command. The younger man must have made a major impression and proved himself an essential asset. When Hawkins's fleet prepared for its second outing in 1567, Drake now had his own ship, the *Judith*. All seemed to go well until the disaster in the harbor of San Juan de Ulúa.

Facts Amid the Hype

This and Drake's later adventures have become part history, part folklore. Sometimes it is difficult to separate the two. One reason is that the English government sometimes lied in its public statements about Drake. The Queen wanted the Spaniards to fear Drake as much as possible. That way, they would waste large amounts of resources and time trying to hunt him down. So English officials frequently exaggerated his accomplishments.

Similarly, Drake wanted to **inflate** his own image. Doing so would make him seem more talented and impressive. So at times he claimed to have taken more captives or valuables than he actually did.

One of several surviving paintings of Queen Elizabeth I, decked out in her finest attire.

Still, some facts can be detected amid the hype. One is that Drake was often kind to, and generous with, his captives. Some of them later admitted that he had treated them with respect and kept them safe from harm.

He even gave them gifts. In 1579, for instance, Drake captured a Spanish ship off the coast of South America. He gave the captain a handsome and quite expensive firearm. That Spaniard later recalled that Drake "had gotten it from Germany and that he prized it highly."[2] Such decent treatment of his adversaries set Drake apart from other pirates and privateers of his day.

For the Glory of God

One reason why Francis Drake treated most of his captives well was that he was a deeply religious man. Modern scholars have found abundant evidence for this. First, his father was a zealous Protestant preacher who drilled his beliefs into his young son. Also, when on the high seas Drake led his crew in prayers twice each day. This was so important to him that he had any sailor who skipped a session whipped.

In addition, in 1556, Drake converted a shipmate named Michael Morgan to the Protestant faith by teaching him about key church laws and writings. In turn, that young man brought an older man into the Protestant fold.

Still other evidence for Drake's religious devotion is seen in surviving letters. One is addressed to one of Drake's friends, Reverend John Fox, and dated April 27, 1587. "I shall desire you," Drake wrote, "to continue a faithful memory of me in your prayers." That way, our deeds may ensure that "God may be glorified" and "his church, our queen, and [our] country [may be] preserved." Also, "the enemies of the truth [will be] so vanquished [defeated] that we may have continual peace." Drake signed the letter, "Your loving and faithful son in Christ Jesus, Francis Drake."[3]

Rev. John Fox in the 1580s

This illustration from the late 1500s shows an English warship similar to the kind Drake commanded.

Daring Adventures in Panama

During their brush with death at San Juan de Ulúa, Drake and Hawkins lost most of the slaves they had obtained in Africa. So they had little to show for their time-consuming and expensive expedition. Drake naturally wanted to offset his losses. And he saw that raiding Spanish ships and towns was a workable way of doing that. It would also give him opportunities to make a name for himself as a bold sea captain.

Drake demonstrated such boldness in voyage after voyage in the Spanish Main. One of the more memorable examples occurred early in 1571 off the coast of Panama, one of Spain's richest colonies. It was frequently a target of pirates.

One day Drake sighted a Spanish trading ship anchored by itself. He ordered an attack on the vessel. But the Spaniards were well-armed and fought hard. They were able to stop Drake's men from boarding and taking the cargo.

At some point, someone cut the anchor cable, which caused the Spanish ship to drift ashore. The crew and passengers swiftly abandoned their vessel and ran away into the woods. That allowed the English to loot the ship at will. While this was happening, Drake wrote a long note and left it onboard when he departed. Viewed as very daring and **impudent** by the Spanish, it read in part, "We are surprised you ran from us in that fashion." The crew and passengers should not have "refused to come and talk to us under our flag of truce." After all, Drake said, "we do ill to no one under our flag of truce." Because "you will not come courteously to talk with us," you will find your ship plundered "by your own fault!"[1]

The Treasure House of the World

While some Spaniards came to admire Drake for his boldness and sense of humor, most hated and feared him for robbing their vessels and towns. His first major success in looting the Spaniards occurred in 1572 when he returned to Panama.

Drake's interest in Panama was due to its special geographic position between the Pacific Ocean and the Caribbean. The Spanish had conquered a large portion of South America, which they called Peru. They shipped the vast stores of silver they collected in Peru northward to southern Panama. From there, mule trains carried the treasure to Nombre de Dios, a prosperous town on Panama's Caribbean shore. Spanish ships picked up the treasure there and took it to Cuba and finally to Spain.

Drake could have attacked the ships on their way to Cuba. But they were extremely well-guarded because the Spaniards fully expected pirates to assault those ships. However, Drake realized, they did *not* expect an attempt to take the treasure while it was on land inside Panama. He hatched an **audacious** plan to make just such an attempt.

The scheme was to launch a predawn assault on Nombre de Dios while the treasure was temporarily stored there. The English crept ashore not far from the town on July 29, 1572. "We arrived there," Drake later wrote, "by three of the clock after midnight," or 3 a.m. "The town took alarm," he went on, "as we perceived" from "the noise and cries of the people" and "the bell ringing out."[2]

As Drake told it, he and his men engaged the Spanish guards in a fierce battle in the town square. Driving the Spaniards away, the English reached the house where the treasure was stored. They saw many bars of silver inside. And the excited Drake shouted to his men that he "had brought them to the mouth of the Treasure House of the world."[3]

A 1672 engraving of the harbor of Nombre de Dios, with the town in the distance.

Another Daring Move

The English were about to gather up the silver when Drake was suddenly hit in the leg by a gunshot. His men worried that he might die. In their loyalty, they switched their focus from the treasure to him. They begged "him to be content to go with them aboard" the ship, "there to have his wound searched and dressed."[4]

This attempt to grab the Spanish treasure failed, therefore. However, Drake was **undaunted**. He reasoned that the enemy would think him foolish to try to steal the treasure on land again. His instincts proved dead right. In another daring move, the following year (1573) he doubled back. Sneaking ashore again, he and his men ambushed a mule train carrying the latest haul of treasure. They made off with most of the silver and gold. And soon the name Francis Drake was on the lips of people across the known world.

An old Spanish sailing ship appears on a modern postage stamp.

Did Drake Give an Honest Account?

Drake described his first attempt to seize the treasure in 1572 in writing. This and other tales about his adventures were later collected into a book. Published several years after his death, it is titled *Sir Francis Drake Revived*.

It is only natural to wonder if he was honest about why this first effort to acquire the treasure failed. Most historians think he was not.

He was "guilty of straying from the truth,"[5] states Michael Turner, an expert on Drake's life. "He writes that when he was wounded" in the leg, "his men loved him so much that they chose to abort the raid on the treasure house and carried him back to the boat."[6]

However, there is evidence that Drake attacked Nombre de Dios at the wrong time. He did not realize that the treasure had passed through the town months before. This suggests that his sources of information were in error. Because that "would have been too embarrassing to admit,"[7] Turner says, Drake lied in his account.

Yet he often made up for that shortcoming by showing a real concern for his shipmates, Turner points out. He "always showed his humble qualities in caring for his men and ships."[8]

Sir Francis Drake
Reuiued : *M. Ireland*.
Calling vpon this Dull or Effeminate Age,
to folowe his Noble Steps for Golde & Siluer,

By this Memorable Relation, of the Rare Occurrances
(neuer yet declared to the World) in a Third Voyage,
made by him into the West-Indies, in the Yeares 72. & 73.
when *Nombre de Dios* was by him and 52. others
only in his Company, surprised.
Faithfully taken out of the Reporte of Mr. *Christofer Ceely, Ellis Hixon*, and others, who were in the same Voyage with him.
By *Philip Nichols*, Preacher.
Reviewed also by Sr. *Francis Drake* himselfe before his Death,
& Much holpen and enlarged, by diuers Notes, with his owne
hand here and there Inserted.
Set forth by Sr. *Francis Drake* Barones
(his Nephew) now liuing.

A photo shows a full-size modern replica of Drake's ship, the Golden Hind.

Drake Sails Around the World

In addition to his exploits as a privateer, Francis Drake was also an accomplished explorer. He led the second expedition in history to **circumnavigate** the world. (The first expedition was led by Ferdinand Magellan and departed in 1519. Magellan died during the voyage but some of his crew returned to their starting point in Spain in 1522.)

A Secret Venture
Early in 1577, one of Queen Elizabeth's advisors approached Drake to propose a new venture that the now-veteran sea captain found extremely exciting. It was also a secret that only the Queen and a few high-placed English officials knew about. They were well aware that Spain had several settlements on the Pacific shores of the Americas. Moreover, rumors claimed that some of those distant towns were rich with gold and silver from Peru. The Queen and her officials told Drake they wanted to acquire as much of that wealth as possible. Taking it would strengthen England, they explained, while weakening Spain. But these places were very far away and difficult to reach. No Englishmen had ever seen them.

The plan's backers drew up top-secret guidelines for Drake to follow. He was to go to "the south sea," meaning the Pacific Ocean, by passing through the strait named

for Magellan near South America's southern tip. Then he should sail "far to the northwards" along the continent's western coast.[1] Along the way, he should raid any rich Spanish towns he could find.

Also, Drake was ordered to "find out [for] the benefit of her majesty's realms, where [people] are not under the obedience of [Spain's king in] hopes of [acquiring] spices, drugs, [etc.]." In other words, Drake should try to open up new trade relations with native peoples in the distant regions he would visit. Finally, the document stated that "Drake [is to] return the same way homewards as he went."[2] Therefore, Drake's orders did not say he should go on a round-the-world voyage. It appears that he decided for himself to pursue that bold goal.

Voyage to California

The expedition left England late in 1577 with five ships. Drake commanded the **flagship**, the *Pelican*. After sailing southward for a while, he captured a Portuguese merchant ship off Africa's western coast and added it to the fleet.

For various reasons, however, Drake lost all of his ships except for the *Pelican*. Once he had made it into the Pacific in September 1588, he renamed the vessel the *Golden Hind*. Then he began a fateful journey up the coast. Reaching the Spanish town of Valparaiso (in modern-day Chile), he looted a gold-laden Spanish ship. In the months that followed, several more Spanish ships surrendered to him. In truth, they had little choice. Because the Spaniards did not expect any enemy attacks in those distant waters, all their ships in that area were unarmed!

Moving much further northward, Drake and his men eventually reached what is now northern California. In mid-June 1579 the *Golden Hind* anchored in a wide inlet not far from modern San Francisco. It is now called Drake's Bay in his honor.

While making routine repairs on the ship, the Englishmen noticed some natives coming to greet them. Francis Fletcher, a Protestant minister who served as the vessel's chaplain, wrote that they had "a loving nature" and lacked any sort of dishonesty. "Their bows and arrows" were used "very skillfully," he added.[3]

Most historians think those natives were members of one of the region's Miwok-speaking tribes. Drake was impressed not only with them but also the area they inhabited. He stayed there for six weeks and claimed the surrounding lands for Queen Elizabeth.

Although the region in question is now largely accepted as the one bordering Drake's Bay, this was not always the case. In fact, for centuries its exact location was unknown and widely debated. Drake made several accurate maps showing his stops. Yet that bay was not on any of the maps released to the public.

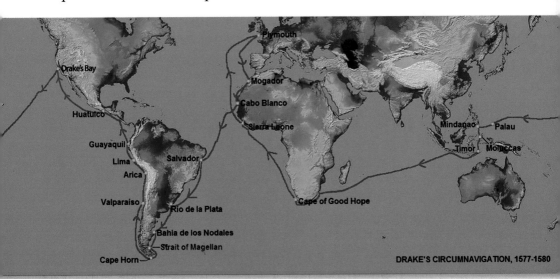

This map shows the route Drake took in his around-the-world voyage.

Return to England

Many modern experts think Drake purposely tried to mislead people. He may have done this in order to keep such valuable information out of Spanish hands. According to this view, he hoped the Queen would send more expeditions to northern California. They would erect settlements there, which might stifle further Spanish expansion in the Americas. It was therefore in England's interest to keep certain key sites a secret.

Whatever Drake was thinking at the time, he seems to have felt that his mission was complete. After leaving the bay in July 1579, he headed west across the Pacific. The *Golden Hind* sailed to Java, in Southeast Asia, and then rounded the African continent. The ship reached England on September 26, 1580.

Drake was now a rich man. He was also a national hero of the first order. So it is not surprising that a few months after he returned, the queen knighted him. From that day forward, he was "Sir" Francis Drake.

A bronze carving portrays Queen Elizabeth knighting Drake in 1580.

The Englishmen as Gods?

Francis Fletcher was not the only person aboard the *Golden Hind* who later wrote an account of the round-the-globe voyage. The other was one of Drake's armed guards, Francis Pretty. He also described the friendly Miwok people, saying in part,

> It pleased God to send us into a fair and good bay, with a good wind to enter the same. In this bay we anchored. And the people of the country, having their houses close by the water's side, showed themselves unto us, and sent a present to our General [Drake]. When they came unto us, they greatly wondered at the things that we brought. But our General, according to his natural and accustomed humanity, courteously . . . bestowed on them necessary things [including clothes] to cover their nakedness. Whereupon [at which point] they supposed us to be gods, and would not be persuaded to the contrary.[4]

Francis Pretty's narrative turned out to be more important than he or Drake could have dreamed. The Miwok were very populous and thriving at the time. Today there are only a little more than 3,500 of them left. Pretty's detailed description provides them with priceless information about their ancestors.

California Indians welcome Drake

A late medieval map shows Santo Domingo at about the time Drake attacked it in 1586.

Several Spanish Cities Plundered

After returning from his circumnavigation, Drake became England's leading celebrity. To get an idea of his fame, imagine if someone today were both a sports hero and a rock star. Part of what thrilled people was Drake's expansion of Europeans' knowledge of the world. No less appealing was that he had returned with loads of Spanish treasure.

One result of Drake's widespread renown was that many members of England's wealthy classes wanted to invest in him. This meant putting up the money to back his next voyage. The common wisdom was that he would surely return with extensive riches. His backers would make a hefty profit.

The First Target: Santiago

Following a lot of deal-making behind the scenes, Drake's next great venture finally became reality in 1585. The Queen led the pack of eager investors. Their money paid for the largest fleet England had ever **mustered**. It consisted of twenty-nine ships and more than 2,300 men. The goal was to raid rich Spanish settlements, especially in the Caribbean region—the so-called West Indies.

The fleet set sail on September 14, 1585. The first target was Santiago, the chief city of the Cape Verde

Islands. Located off Africa's western coast, the islands had been discovered by Portugal in the prior century. In 1580, however, the year Drake returned from his trip around the world, that situation changed. Spain's king, Phillip II, took control of Portugal. The Spaniards now exploited the islands' residents and riches.

Any Spanish outpost was fair game for Drake. His huge fleet arrived at Santiago on November 17 and his men rapidly looted it. To his surprise, however, the spoils consisted mostly of wine, olive oil, and other foodstuffs. These had a certain value. But no gold or silver was found.

Perhaps because of his disappointment at finding no treasure, Drake ordered the town destroyed. "At our departing, we consumed with fire all the houses,"[1] wrote Walter Biggs, one of the English soldiers. His lengthy account of the expedition was published in England four years later.

Hero Worship?

Drake sailed westward and reached Santo Domingo, on the large Spanish island of Hispaniola, on New Year's Day, 1586. The city was "well fortified," Biggs said. Particularly impressive was "a castle" that was "furnished with a great store of **artillery**."[2]

But its "store" of artillery wasn't "great" enough. Drake's men overwhelmed the defenses. After plundering Santo Domingo, Drake moved on to Cartagena, on South America's northern coast. He captured it on February 9, 1586 and seized all its valuables. To their credit, Biggs wrote, the Spaniards put up a valiant fight. For hours, fierce hand-to-hand fighting raged in the streets. "They had raised very fine *barricades*," Biggs continued. These consisted "of earthworks with trenches" dug around them.[3]

Finally, Drake sailed northward to St. Augustine, in what is now northern Florida. He captured and destroyed the town between May 28 and 30. He made it back to England two months later.

Biggs's account of the expedition bore the lengthy title *A Summary and True Discourse of Sir Francis Drake's West Indian Voyage, Begun in the Year 1585*. It was widely popular in England. Most of those who read it came away thinking Drake's voyage had been a big success. But was the expedition as successful as Biggs made it out to be? Throughout the narrative, he described Drake's orders

This fortress in St. Augustine still looks largely as it did when Drake raided the town.

and decisions in positive terms. Indeed, at times the words amounted to hero worship. Drake was usually called "the general." And Biggs described him planning complex land-based attacks on towns. This made it seem as though Drake was a trained leader of land armies, like the famous ancient generals Alexander the Great and Julius Caesar. It is true that Drake was a skilled commander. But his talents lay mainly in ships and other naval matters.

Some Bad Decisions

The book also made it look like Drake was a great champion of the common people. Any person who was "for the common benefit of the people and country," Biggs wrote, should "come and present himself unto our noble and merciful governor, Sir Francis Drake."[4] The reality, however, was quite different. Drake's famed generosity and good humor were reserved mainly for members of the wealthy and noble classes. As modern biographer Harry Kelsey points out, Drake was usually not so nice to poorer common folk. For the most part, "he treated the ordinary sailors with **contempt**," or scorn. In fact, he frequently "punished them severely for the slightest" mistake.[5]

Finally, Biggs's book suggested that the expedition had been a big financial success. But this was untrue. Drake made some bad decisions and missed several opportunities. As a result, he brought back far less money than the venture's backers had hoped for. The English government praised the expedition in public to keep up people's confidence in their leaders. But such praise was largely phony. In a private meeting, those leaders called the voyage "not so good a success as was hoped for."[6] This shows that surviving sources that regularly praise Drake cannot always be trusted.

Biggs's Account Explained

Walter Biggs's account provides a detailed and exciting depiction of the fight for Cartagena. However, some of the words in his account are no longer commonly used today.

For example, he said that Drake's men were "well furnished with pikes and shots." By this, he meant that many of them had extremely long spears, then called pikes. At the time, "shots" was a slang word for the ammunition for early, bulky hand-held guns.

A typical formation of soldiers on the battlefield consisted of a big square of pikemen, with gunners guarding its sides. This array was regularly called "pikes and shots."

"Our pikes were somewhat longer than theirs, and our bodies better armed," Biggs continued. Thanks to this advantage, the enemy had no choice but to "give place," or retreat. Soon Drake's second-in-command "slew with his own hands the chief ensign-bearer of the Spaniards." Ensigns were a military unit's flags and banners. To his credit, that flag-carrier "fought very manfully to his life's end."

Then Drake's forces entered the town, giving the enemy "no leisure to breathe," or no chance to rest. Biggs said that the Spaniards were defeated because they were "not able to endure the fury of such a hot assault," or forceful attack.[7]

In the battle for Cartagena, the English used a square formation of pikemen like this one.

A painting shows English warships fighting the Spanish Armada in 1588.

Attack of the Spanish Armada

Ⱥ ot long after his expedition to the West Indies, Drake took part in another major seafaring adventure. Like several earlier ones, it involved attacking Spanish ships. But this time he was defending his homeland against invasion.

That would-be invasion came about because of serious disagreements between Queen Elizabeth and Spain's king, Philip II. Philip asked Elizabeth to marry him and unite their countries. But she refused, which made him angry. Elizabeth also refused to halt the attacks on Spanish vessels and colonies by Drake and other English sea captains. Finally, the two monarchs differed in religious matters. Philip was a devout Catholic. And it greatly annoyed him that under Elizabeth England was predominately a Protestant country.

Philip came to feel that there was only one way to resolve these differences. He must conquer England. To that end, he ordered Spain's Duke of Medina Sidonia to prepare an enormous fleet of warships. It became known as the Spanish Armada.

An Awesome and Frightening Sight
English spies revealed what was happening in Spain. Elizabeth knew she must at all costs stop the Armada from reaching English shores. Part of the plan was to add new warships to England's fleet. In a letter to the queen and her

advisors, Drake said those ships had to be many in number. And the vessels must carry as many cannons as could be mustered. "The advantage of time and place," Drake added, was also crucial. "I hold it in my poor opinion the surest and best course."[1]

That best course, Drake explained, was to take a squadron of ships to Spain and stop its massive fleet from sailing. He sailed into the Spanish harbor of Cádiz in April 1587 and achieved complete surprise. He sank about 30 ships. But his raid didn't end the threat. In May 1588, the 131 warships of the Spanish Armada departed for England. They carried more than 17,000 troops. The plan

One of several portraits of Spain's King Philip II by the noted Italian artist Titian (c. 1488–1576).

was for them, along with 30,000 Spanish soldiers then in the Netherlands, to land in southern England and march on London.

The Armada in full sail was an awesome and frightening sight to behold. An Italian named Juan Bentivollo saw it from a distance and wrote,

> You could hardly see the sea. The Spanish fleet was stretched out in the form of a half moon with an immense distance between its [ends]. [It] caused horror mixed with wonder. . . . [The fleet] came on with a steady and deliberate movement, yet when it drew near in full sail it seemed almost that the waves groaned under its weight and the winds were made to obey it.[2]

The Angry Duke

As that enormous fleet moved slowly northward toward England, the queen named four men to command her own naval forces. They were Drake, John Hawkins, Lord Charles Howard, and veteran sea captain Martin Frobisher. Drake commanded the *Revenge*, with a crew of 250. He and his fellow admirals had about two hundred ships. That was almost seventy more than the Spaniards. However, the Spanish vessels were much larger and harder to sink than the English ships.

The two fleets engaged each other in a series of battles at the end of July. On the first day, Drake followed the English plan. He attacked the left end of the Spaniards' vast half-moon, or **crescent**, formation. Meanwhile, other English ships moved against the right end.

Two of the Spanish ships broke their formation. They tried to destroy some English vessels. But because the English ships were smaller than the Spanish ones, they were also faster and more maneuverable. The two Spanish ships were surrounded and the Duke of Medina Sidonia had to rescue them. He angrily issued a new order. "It is of great importance," he said, "that the Armada should be kept well together." He added, "no ship belonging to the Armada shall separate from it without my permission . . . any disobedience of this order shall be punished by death."[3]

The next day, the Duke had even more to be angry about. Drake managed to capture one of the giant Spanish ships. It was the *Rosario*, which had been disabled in a collision. Even more embarrassing for the Spaniards, Drake discovered a large **cache** of gold aboard the vessel.

Saved by the Weather?

Due in part to the skill and courage of the English sea captains and sailors, the Spanish attempt to invade England failed. As a result, King Philip's plans were spoiled. And the Duke of Medina Sidonia was disgraced. Indeed, for the rest of his life the Duke was taunted by children in the streets. "Look out!" they cried out, "Drake is coming!"[4]

That made it seem like Drake had a lot to do with the Armada's failure. Yet the size of Drake's role in the Spaniards' defeat remains unclear. There is no doubt that he did capture the *Rosario* and its treasure. Beyond that and a couple of other documented episodes, little is known about his deeds during the battles with the Armada.

The fact is that on July 30 the wind changed to a southerly direction. That forced the Spaniards to head northward rather than being able to return the way they had come. Storms took an awful toll on them. Less than half the original armada made it back to Spain. Drake was brave and bold, to be sure. But it appears that the weather may have done more to save England from invasion than he did.

A Divine Victory?

The major change in wind direction on July 30, 1588, is today given much of the credit for the Spanish Armada's defeat. Interestingly, both the Spanish and English leaders recognized that fact at the time. Drake himself is said to have remarked: "There was never anything pleased me better than seeing the enemy flying with a southerly wind northward."[5]

Not long after the Spanish galleons headed north, a succession of storms battered them. Many of King Philip's sailors drowned. Others managed to scramble ashore, only to be killed by vengeful locals.

The surviving Spanish ships eventually returned to their homeland. Their captains faced the unhappy King Philip. He told them, "I sent you out to war with men, not with the wind and waves." These words show he knew that their mission was ruined mostly by the weather.

In England, by contrast, Queen Elizabeth called the change of weather the "Protestant wind." In her view, God had clearly sided with her Protestant nation. So she had a special medal made to mark the supposedly divine victory. The medal bore the words "God blew and they were scattered."[6] Here, the word *they* refers to the Spanish ships.

Francis Drake in Popular Culture

The fight against the Spanish Armada turned out to be the last of Drake's successful adventures. Never again would he enjoy the kind of personal triumphs he had achieved earlier in his memorable career. In 1589, the year after the Armada's defeat, the queen gave him a new assignment. He and military commander John Norris journeyed to Portugal, hoping to help Portuguese leaders break away from Spanish control. But the expedition largely failed.

In the End: A Soldier!
A few years later, in 1595, Drake left England on still another naval campaign. This time he was accompanied by his cousin and former partner John Hawkins. The two had long since patched up their differences and agreed to work together in harmony. Such cooperation was essential because the new venture was complex and dangerous.

The objective was to capture a Spanish treasure ship then under repairs in the harbor of San Juan, Puerto Rico. The two English captains hoped to catch the Spanish by surprise. But this was not to be. Gone were the days when Spain's colonies in the Americas were unprepared for attacks by pirates and other attackers. Drake and Hawkins found San Juan both well-prepared and well defended. So they were unable to capture the treasure ship.

Next, Drake tried to attack Spanish ports in Panama. There, he intended to stop enemy shipments of gold and silver from Peru once and for all. Once again, however, the Spaniards were well-fortified and ready to repel an assault. The expedition failed.

Drake was still off Panama's coast when he contracted **dysentery**, an infection of the intestines. Several of his crewmen had already died of it. Sensing he had little time left, he donned his armor, intending to look the part of a soldier when the end came. He died on January 28, 1596. Following his instructions, his crew placed him in a lead coffin and lowered it into the sea off Panama's coast.

Devil or Hero?

Drake left behind a striking **legacy**. But the nature of that legacy depends on who did the remembering. To the Spanish and some other Europeans, Drake left behind a dark legacy. He had sunk many Spanish vessels and killed thousands of Spaniards. So in Spain and its colonies, he was a devil-like character. As Harry Kelsey says, Spaniards "described Drake as a man of terrifying stature." He was "an enemy of their king and their church . . . the name of Francis Drake came to represent the English enemy."[1]

To the English, in contrast, Drake was a national hero. That was also the case for future English colonies. So in countries like the United States, originally an English colony, Drake retains his heroic stature.

In England in particular, people long remembered him with affection and even awe. Legends grew up about him. One legend claimed that if the English were ever threatened with destruction, they should beat on a drum

while chanting his name. He would awaken and return to save the nation. This is a version of a type of folktale called the "sleeping hero." (Another version of it claims that the medieval champion King Arthur will someday awaken and save England.)

Drake's legacy in England also includes the frequent naming of places after him. In and around Plymouth, where he grew up, a naval base, an island, and a shopping mall all bear his name. A similar situation exists in the western United States, from the widespread belief that he landed in California during his round-the-world voyage. Drake's Bay is one example. San Francisco has a street named Sir Francis Drake Boulevard.

From Plays to Video Games

Drake's memory as a hero has been exploited in the media. In the early 1930s, British playwright Louis M. Parker wrote *Drake of England*. It was made into a movie in 1935, with Canadian actor Matheson Lang as Drake. In 1961, a British TV series called *Sir Francis Drake* became popular. An American television movie, *The Immortal Voyage of Captain Drake*, was released in 2009. Drake has even inspired video games. *Uncharted: Drake's Fortune* stars an imaginary great-great- (and many more greats) grandson of Drake named Nathan Drake. He searches for gold that his ancestor supposedly found during his voyage around the world.

In short, Francis Drake's lust for life and valiant spirit live on. In countless ways, people remember him primarily either as a thieving pirate or a great patriot. Which of these is more accurate will likely never be known. Too many of his deeds and words are forever lost. They lie somewhere in that hazy area that floats between the realms of legend and reality.

Suing for Drake's Treasure

Plays, movies, TV shows, and video games are not the only aspects of popular culture inspired by Drake's memory. In 1919, an American **con artist** named Oscar Hartzell began using Drake's name to cheat people.

A resident of Iowa, Hartzell found many Iowans with the last name of Drake. He convinced them that they were distant relatives of Sir Francis Drake. Drake had left behind a huge fortune now supposedly worth billions of dollars, Hartzell claimed. He also said the British government still held that money.

These were bold-faced lies. Yet Hartzell insisted that all he needed was enough money to sue Britain, which would fork over the treasure. All of those modern-day Drakes would share the money.

Incredibly, tens of thousands of people believed Hartzell and gave him their life savings. He ran off to London and for years lived like a king. Law enforcement officers managed to catch up with him in the 1930s and plunked him in jail. But some of the people he had duped continued to send him money until the day he died!

This bronze statue of Drake stands in Plymouth, England.

Chapter Notes

Introduction: Betrayal and a Longing for Revenge

1. Zelia Nuttall, *New Light on Drake* (London: Hakluyt Society, 1914), p. 301.

2. Hans P. Kraus, "Sir Francis Drake: A Pictorial Biography: The Unfortunate Voyage to San Juan de Ulua, 1567-1569." http://www.loc.gov/rr/rarebook/catalog/drake/drake-1-actors.html

3. Ibid.

4. Ibid.

5. Richard Hakluyt, *Principal Navigations, Voyages, and Discoveries of the English Nation* (London: George Bishop and Ralph Newberie, 1589), p. 556.

Chapter 1: Learning to Be a Ship's Captain

1. Chelsea C. Curtis, *Boys' Book of Sea Fights* (Charleston, SC: BiblioBazaar, 2010), p. 4.

2. Michael Turner, "The Real Francis Drake." http://www.indrakeswake.co.uk/Drake/realdrake.htm

3. British Library, London. *Harley Manuscript* 7002, folio 8.

Chapter 2: Daring Adventures in Panama

1. Irene A. Wright, *Spanish Documents Concerning English Voyages to the Caribbean, 1527-1568* (London: Hakluyt Society, 1929), p. 11.

2. Francis Drake, *Sir Francis Drake Revived*, ed. Philip Nichols. http://www.gutenberg.org/files/2854/2854-h/2854-h.htm

3. Ibid.

4. Ibid.

5. Michael Turner, "The Real Francis Drake." http://www.indrakeswake.co.uk/Drake/realdrake.htm

6. Ibid.

7. Ibid.

8. Ibid.

Chapter 3: Drake Sails Around the World

1. Harry Kelsey. *Sir Francis Drake: The Queen's Pirate* (New Haven, CT: Yale University Press, 1998), p. 77.

2. Ibid., p. 78.

3. Francis Fletcher, *The World Encompassed by Sir Francis Drake* (London: Hakluyt Society, 1854), p. 131.

Chapter Notes

4. Modern History Sourcebook. *Francis Pretty: Sir Francis Drake's Voyage Round the World, 1580.* http://www.fordham.edu/halsall/mod/1580Pretty-drake.asp

Chapter 4: Several Spanish Cities Plundered

1. Walter Biggs. A *Summary and True Discourse of Sir Francis Drake's West Indian Voyage, Begun in the Year 1585.* Published by Project Gutenberg as "Drake's Great Armada." http://www.gutenberg.org/files/3334/3334-h/3334-h.htm

2. Ibid.

3. Ibid.

4. Ibid.

5. Harry Kelsey. *Sir Francis Drake: The Queen's Pirate* (New Haven, CT: Yale University Press, 1998), p. 278.

6. John R. Dasent, ed. *Acts of the Privy Council of England,* vol. 15 (Norwich, England: Her Majesty's Stationery Office, 1899), pp. 76-77.

7. Biggs, *A Summary and True Discourse.*

Chapter 5: Attack of the Spanish Armada

1. Letter from Francis Drake to Queen Elizabeth 1, April 13, 1588. Public Records Office, London: State Papers, 12/209/89, folio 134v.

2. John Simkin, "The Spanish Armada." Spartacus International. http://spartacus-educational.com/TUDarmada.htm

3. Martin A.S. Hume, ed., *Calendar of Letters and State Papers Relating to English Affairs,* vol. 4 (London: Her Majesty's Stationery Office, 1899), p. 291.

4. Ernle Bradford, *The Wind Commands Me: A Life of Sir Francis Drake* (New York: Harcourt Brace, 1965), p. 224.

5. The Elizabeth Files, "Spanish Armada 5." http://www.elizabethfiles.com/the-spanish-armada-5-the-protestant-wind/4029/

6. The Elizabeth Files, "Spanish Armada 9." http://www.elizabethfiles.com/spanish-armada-9-god-blew-and-they-were-scattered/4097/

Chapter 6: Francis Drake in Popular Culture

1. Harry Kelsey, *Sir Francis Drake: The Queen's Pirate* (New Haven: Yale University Press, 1998), p. 398.

Works Consulted

Bawlf, Samuel. *The Secret Voyage of Sir Francis Drake, 1577–1580*. New York: Penguin, 2004.

Bradford, Ernle. *The Wind Commands Me: A Life of Sir Francis Drake*. New York: Harcourt Brace, 1965.

Drake, Francis. *Sir Francis Drake Revived*, ed. Philip Nichols. http://www.gutenberg.org/files/2854/2854-h/2854-h.htm

Fletcher, Francis. *The World Encompassed by Sir Francis Drake*. London: Hakluyt Society, 1854.

Hakluyt, Richard. *Principal Navigations, Voyages, and Discoveries of the English Nation*. London: George Bishop and Ralph Newberie, 1589.

Hutchinson, Robert. *The Spanish Armada*. New York: Thomas Dunne, 2014.

Kelsey, Harry. *Sir Francis Drake: The Queen's Pirate*. New Haven, CT: Yale University Press, 1998.

Konstam, Angus. *Elizabethan Sea Dogs, 1560-1605*. London: Osprey, 2000.

Konstam, Angus. *The Great Expedition: Sir Francis Drake on the Spanish Main, 1585-1586*. London: Osprey, 2007.

Kraus, Hans P. "Sir Francis Drake: A Pictorial Biography: The Unfortunate Voyage to San Juan de Ulua, 1567-1569." http://www.loc.gov/rr/rarebook/catalog/drake/drake-1-actors.html

Marrin, Albert. *The Sea King: Sir Francis Drake and His Times*. New York: Atheneum, 1995.

Modern History Sourcebook. *Francis Pretty: Sir Francis Drake's Voyage Round the World, 1580*. http://www.fordham.edu/halsall/mod/1580Pretty-drake.asp

Nuttall, Zelia. *New Light on Drake*. London: Hakluyt Society, 1914.

Sugden, John. *Sir Francis Drake*. New York: Random House, 2012.

Turner, Michael. "The Real Francis Drake." http://www.indrakeswake.co.uk/Drake/realdrake.htm

Viles, Donald M. *Francis Drake in the New World*. Newport, OR: Dancing Moon Press, 2007.

Whitfield, Peter. *Sir Francis Drake*. New York: New York University Press, 2004.

Wright, Irene A. *Spanish Documents Concerning English Voyages to the Caribbean, 1527–1568*. London: Hakluyt Society, 1929.

Further Reading

Childs, Rob. *The Story of Sir Francis Drake*. London: Wayland, 2008.

Crompton, Samuel W. *Sir Francis Drake and the Oceans of the World*. New York: Chelsea House, 2006.

Konstam, Angus. *World Atlas of Pirates*. Guilford, CT: Globe Pequot Press, 2009.

Krull, Kathleen. *Lives of the Pirates*. Boston: Harcourt, 2010.

Nich, Charles. *Sir Francis Drake: Slave Trader and Pirate*. New York: Franklin Watts, 2009.

Petcher, Kenneth. *Explorers of the Late Renaissance and the Enlightenment: From Sir Francis Drake to Mungo Park*. New York: Rosen, 2011.

Pratt, Mary K. *Elizabeth I: English Renaissance Queen*. Edina, MN: ABDO, 2011.

On the Internet

"A Brief History of Piracy." Royal Naval Museum.
http://www.royalnavalmuseum.org/info_sheets_piracy.htm

"Francis Drake." Britannia Biographies.
http://www.britannia.com/bios/gents/fdrake.html

"Francis Drake." British Empire: Explorers.
http://www.britishempire.co.uk/biography/francisdrake.htm

"Francis Drake." History Channel.
http://www.history.com/topics/exploration/francis-drake

"Sir Francis Drake." Royal Museums Greenwich.
http://www.rmg.co.uk/explore/sea-and-ships/facts/explorers-and-leaders/drake

"Francis Drake." Spartacus Educational.
http://spartacus-educational.com/TUDdrakeF.htm

Michael Turner, "In Drake's Wake."
http://www.indrakeswake.co.uk/

"Queen Elizabeth I." British Royal Family History.
http://www.britroyals.com/kings.asp?id=elizabeth1

"The Spanish Armada." British Battles.com.
http://www.britishbattles.com/spanish-war/spanish-armada.htm

Glossary

armada (ar-MAH-duh)—a very large fleet of ships

artillery (ar-TILL-er-ee)—cannons and other large guns

audacious (aw-DAY-shuss)—very bold, brave, or daring

cache (CASH)—a group of objects in storage

circumnavigate (sir-cum-NA-vuh-gait)—to travel all the way around something, often a reference to going around the world

con artist (CAWN AR-tist)—person who tries to trick others into giving him or her their money

crescent (KRES-uhnt)—curved or half-moon shape

dysentery (DIS-in-tare-ee)—an infection of the intestines that can cause repeated cases of diarrhea and, if left untreated, can lead to serious illness and even death

flagship (FLAG-ship)—the lead vessel in a fleet of ships

gun (GUN)—when used as a naval term, a cannon

impudent (IM-pue-dent)—rude or disrespectful

inflate (in-FLATE)—to make something bigger

legacy (LEG-uh-see)—memories of one's exploits handed down to future generations

lucrative (LOO-kruh-tiv)—profitable or worthwhile

muster (MUH-ster)—to gather together or collect

negotiate (nuh-GO-shee-ate)—to discuss something in hopes of making a deal

privateer (prie-vuh-TIER)—a person, usually a sea captain, who makes war on an enemy at the request of his own government

treachery (TRECH-er-ee)—betrayal or deceit

undaunted (un-DAWN-tid)—fearless

Index

About the Author

Historian and award-winning writer Don Nardo has published more than four hundred and fifty books for teens and children, along with a number of volumes for college and general adult readers. Many of these volumes are about the peoples of the ancient world and their cultures. Others deal with colorful characters in medieval and early modern times, including explorers, soldiers, inventors and pirates. Mr. Nardo also composes and arranges orchestral music. He lives with his wife Christine in Massachusetts.